Diet recommendations for TCM - Large intestine - heat blocks the colon II acutely

Please check these recommendations always with a nutrition consultant, therapist, doctor or dietician. The recipes and the list of ingredients are supporting the conventional medical therapy.
The calorie disclosures of fresh ingredients (fruit and vegetables) vary according to quality and time of harvest. The contents were checked by a dietician and a nutrition consultant for the Traditional Chinese Medicine (TCM).

Author:
©2019 Josef Miligui
www.ebns.at

AF206911

Source:
The lists are created from the EBNS database for nutritional counseling. The database is used by dietitians, therapists and doctors for advising the patient / client.

Literature:
The specialist literature and the training documents of the German and Austrian dietary and traditional Chinese medicine serve as a knowledge base. We have used the documents as a basis of knowledge, adapted it to our experience and completed them.
http://di-book.com

Production and publishing:
BoD – Books on Demand, Norderstedt
ISBN: 9783746096490

Diet recommendations for TCM - Large intestine - heat blocks the colon II acutely

1   Treatment strategy

Eliminate heat in stomach and colon, promote stool, supplement fluids.

2   Avoid

n.a.

3   Breakfast

	kkal. per serving
Banana Soymilk	125
Blueberry puree	10
Carrot and rice gruel soup	101
Carrot drink	143
Celery juice	33
Corn coffee with cardamom	3
Cottage cheese with steamed fruit	214
Cranberry yogurt mix	57
Curdcheesedumplings on strawberry pulp	553
Fennel-Rice Soup	155
Hot water with grape juice	87
Kohlrabi Potatoes mash	278
Mashed banana	144
Olive oil with lemon juice	93
Pear compote	100
Potato pancakes	893
Potato-basil soup	95
Rhubarb and apple jelly	180
Rice congee with carrots and fennel	131
Rice with parsnips	206
Rosemary Potatoes	188
Semolina porridge with banana	307
Spring vegetables	63
Tea from anise	2
Tea from coriander	2
Tea from elderberry blossom tea	7
Tea from fenugreek (Trigonella foenum-graecum)	0
Tea from marjoram	0
Vanilla pudding	254
Vegetable semolina soup	198

4 Snack

5 Lunch

6   Afternoon

7   Dinner

8 Any time

9 Recipes

(rec.) = You can use more.
(little) = You should use less than specified
(omit) = omit.

9.1 Banana Soymilk

Promotes stomach-spleen harmony, moisturizes, builds up Yin, reduces internal heat, moisturizes intestines, forces stomach and kidneys Yin.
Cooking time approx. 5 min
Calories p. portion: 126
2 portions
Allergens: E

Quantity of ingredients:
Banana 1 piece / 120g. (rec.) - cool - sweet, rough....................................earth
Soybean milk 1 1/2 cups / 400g. (little) - cool - sweet ....earth
Honey 1 teaspoon / 3g. (little) - cold - sweet ....earth
Cinnamon ground 1 pinch / 1g. (yes) - hot - acrid, sweet............................... *
Acerola fruit nectar or powder 1 teaspoon / 2g. (little) - warm - sour......... wood

Cooking instructions:
Cut the banana into pieces, puree them with soy milk, acerola, honey and cinnamon with the mixing stick.

9.2 Basic recipe for a beef broth (clear)

Strengthens Qi and Yang, is very warming.
Cooking time approx. 4-8 hours
Calories p. portion: 114
10 portions
Allergens: O

Quantity of ingredients:
Beef soup meat 1,1 lbs / 500g. (little) - warm - sweet ....earth
Beef meatbones 5/8 oz / 200g. (little) - warm - sweet ....earth
Vinegar (Red wine vinegar) 1 dash / 3g. (little) - warm - sour, bitter .... wood
Juniper berry 8 pieces / 6g. (yes) - warm - sweet, acrid, bitter.....................fire
Rosemary 1 pinch / 1g. (yes) - warm - bitter ....fire
Carrot 3 pieces / 210g. (rec.) - neutral - sweet..earth
Parsnip 2 pieces / 300g. (yes) - cool - bitter ....fire
Leek 1 piece / 200g. (omit) - warm - acrid.. metal
Ginger fresh 1/2 teaspoon / 5g. (omit) - warm - acrid.............................. metal
Lovage 1 stem / 15g. (rec.) - warm - acrid, bitter....................................... metal

Clove 2 pieces / 2g. (yes) - warm - acrid .... metal
Pimento 6 pieces / 12g. (yes) - hot - acrid .... metal
Anise (Common Fennel) 2 pieces / 1g. (rec.) - warm - acrid .... earth
Salt 1 teaspoon / 5g. (little) - cold - salty .... water
Water 3,3 lbs / 1300g. (yes) - cool - salty .... earth

Cooking instructions:
Heat water, a dash of red wine vinegar, some juniper berries, a little rosemary, bones and meat till it boils; add carrot, parsnip, leek, ginger, lovage, clove, allspice, star anise and a little salt; simmer for 4-8 hours then strain.
Refrigerate for later use.

9.3   Basic recipe for a fish broth

Strengthens kidney Qi and Yin, strengthens blood and fluids, promotes urination.
Cooking time approx. 40 min
Calories p. portion: 128
5 portions
Allergens: DLO

Quantity of ingredients:
Fish pieces mixed 3/4 lbs / 300g. (yes) - warm - sweet, salty .... water
Celery root 1/4 lbs - 4oz / 120g. (rec.) - cool - sweet .... earth
Leek 2 inches / 10g. (omit) - warm - acrid .... metal
Carrot 2 pieces / 150g. (rec.) - neutral - sweet .... earth
White wine 1/2 cup / 125g. (omit) - cool - sweet, bitter, acrid .... wood
Lemon 1/2 piece / 50g. (omit) - cold - sour .... wood
Bay leaf 2 leaves / 2g. (yes) - warm - acrid .... metal
Peppercorns 3 pieces / 2g. (omit) - warm - acrid .... metal
Olive oil 1 table spoon / 10g. (little) - cool - sweet .... earth
Water 2 cup / 450g. (yes) - cool - salty .... earth

Cooking instructions:
Fry celery, chopped carrots and leeks in olive oil, add bay leaf and peppercorns, add pieces of fish and sauté briefly. Add water, add little white wine or lemon. Simmer gently for 30 minutes. Skim off the resulting foam several times. In the end, sift the ingredients through a cloth.
Refrigerate for later use

9.4 Basic recipe for a reissue soup (Congee)

Warms the stomach and spleen, harmonizes the intestine, forces Qi, reduces moisture.
Cooking time approx. 2-4 hours
Calories p. portion: 140
3 portions

Quantity of ingredients:
Rice variety any 1 cup / 120g. (yes) - warm - sweet.................................metal
Water 6 cups / 700g. (yes) - cool - salty...earth

Cooking instructions:
Cook rice and water in a ratio of about 1: 6. The amount of water determines the thickness of the mash (matter of taste).
Put the rice in a saucepan with a heavy lid. It is important to simmer the rice after a short boil on the slightest flame, otherwise it burns.
Boil the rice for 2-4 hours. The longer it cooks, the more it strengthens. If you want to eat the dish for breakfast, you can put the rice on just before bedtime.
To be on the safe side, you should first check the behavior of your pot and cooker under observation for a similar amount of time, so that nothing burns.
Refrigerate for later use.

9.5 Basic recipe for a vegetable soup, nutritious

Strengthens spleen and lung, regulates Qi flow, builds up Qi, dries out, passes downwardly, strengthens stomach Qi.
Cooking time approx. 2-3 hours
Calories p. portion: 48
5 portions
Allergens: L

Quantity of ingredients:
Olive oil 1 table spoon / 4g. (little) - cool - sweet...................................earth
Onion white 1 piece / 60g. (omit) - warm - acrid.......................................metal
Carrot 3 pieces / 200g. (rec.) - neutral - sweet.......................................earth
Parsnip 3/8 lbs - 6oz / 150g. (yes) - cool - bitter.......................................fire
Celery root 1 cup / 100g. (rec.) - cool - sweet ....earth
Ginger fresh 1/2 teaspoon / 2g. (omit) - warm - acrid.............................metal
Lemon 1/2 piece / 25g. (omit) - cold - sour...wood
Juniper berry 6 pieces / 6g. (yes) - warm - sweet, acrid, bitter ....fire
Thyme dried 1 pinch / 1g. (yes) - warm - bitter...metal
Lovage 1 table spoon / 3g. (rec.) - warm - acrid, bitter.............................metal

Bay leaf 2 leaves / 1g. (yes) - warm - acrid .... metal
Salt 1 pinch / 1g. (little) - cold - salty .... water
Water 3 cups / 650g. (yes) - cool - salty...earth

Cooking instructions:
Cut the vegetables into cubes.
Heat oil in hot pot, fry shortly onions and vegetables.
Add cold water, then add ginger, bay leaf and lemon juice.
Season with juniper, thyme and lovage. Cover for 2 - 3 hours on a low heat and simmer.
The used vegetables should be thrown away.
The basic recipe serves as a soup base and to refine vegetables, legumes or cereals.
If you want to eat vegetable soup immediately, add the desired vegetables half an hour before.
Refrigerate for later use.

9.6   Basmati rice + Zucchini tofu dish

Converts mucus, reduces heat, builds up Qi, nourishes fluids, harmonizes spleen and stomach, forces Lungen Qi.
Cooking time approx. 20 min
Calories p. portion: 146
4 portions
Allergens: E

Quantity of ingredients:
Soy Tofu 5/8 lbs - 8oz / 250g. (little) - cool - sweet ....earth
Olive oil 2 table spoons / 6g. (little) - cool - sweet ....earth
Coriander 1/2 teaspoon / 4g. (yes) - warm - acrid....................................metal
Ginger fresh 1/2 teaspoon / 4g. (omit) - warm - acrid...............................metal
Rice Basmati 1/2 cup / 60g. (yes)   neutral - sweet...................................metal
Water 3 cups / 200g. (yes) - cool - salty...earth
Zucchini 1 piece / 700g. (rec.) - cool - sweet...earth

Cooking instructions:
Cut tofu cubes and marinate with olive oil, tamari, crushed coriander and ginger. Leave at least 1 hour.
Cook Basmati rice with the water. You can season with onion and cardamom.
Roast zucchini and tofu in pan in the hot oil for approx. 5-7 min.
Serve rice and tofu on a plate.
Add the parsley.
Can also be used as a salad for the home and on the go.

9.7 Black root with yogurt

Nourishes Yin, relaxes, builds up Qi, moisturizes dryness, preserves the fluids.
Cooking time approx. 20 min
Calories p. portion: 266
2 portions
Allergens: AG

Quantity of ingredients:
Salsify 1 lbs / 400g. (yes) - cool - sweet..earth
Yogurt (natural, 1.5% fat) 4 table spoons / 80g. (yes) - cool - sour .... wood
Salt 1 pinch / 1g. (little) - cold - salty .... water
Multi-grain bread (gray bread) 6 slices / 120g. (little) - cool - sweet .... wood

Cooking instructions:
Peel the salsify and simmer in salted water until tender. Pour away the water, cool the salsify and cut it to size. Cover with yoghurt and sprinkle with fresh herbs. Serve with the bread.
You can also use the salsify from the conserve.

9.8 Blueberry puree

Keeps fluids and essence, forces liver and kidneys, forces blood, forces eyesight, warms spleen- and kidney-
Yang, directs upwards, warms the stomach and spleen, promotes blood circulation and conduction flow, relieves cold-sickness and pain.
Cooking time approx. 10 min
Calories p. portion: 10
1 portion

Quantity of ingredients:
Blueberry 1/2 oz / 20g. (yes) - cool - sweet, sour .... wood
Cinnamon ground 1 pinch / 0,1g. (yes) - hot - acrid, sweet.............................. *
Clove 1 piece / 1g. (yes) - warm - acrid.. metal
Water 1 cup / 250g. (yes) - cool - salty...earth

Cooking instructions:
Boil blueberries with cinnamon and clove in water for 10 minutes. Remove the cinnamon and clove. Puree. Sweet as desired.

9.9 Broccoli cream soup

Nourishes lung Yin, produces humors, strengthens spleen and liver, moisturizes, reduces cold-evil, softens knots.
Cooking time approx. 30 min
Calories p. portion: 98
6 portions
Allergens: LO

Quantity of ingredients:
Olive oil 2 table spoons / 7g. (little) - cool - sweet ....earth
Broccoli 1,1 lbs / 500g. (yes) - cool - sweet...earth
Carrot 2 pieces / 150g. (rec.) - neutral - sweet ....earth
Potato 2 pieces / 120g. (rec.) - neutral - sweet..earth
Onion white 1 piece / 50g. (omit) - warm - acrid...metal
Water 1 cup / 50g. (yes) - cool - salty..earth
Basic recipe for a vegetable soup (nutritious) 2 cup / 500g. (rec.) - neutral - *. *
White wine 1/2 cup / 125g. (omit) - cool - sweet, bitter, acrid ....wood
Sage 1 teaspoon / 2g. (yes) - cool - bitter, spicy ....fire
Rosemary 1 teaspoon / 2g. (yes) - warm - bitter ....fire
Pepper (ground) 1 pinch / 0,5g. () - warm - acrid ....metal
Salt 1 pinch / 1g. (little) - cold - salty ....water

Cooking instructions:
Add the olive oil to the pan, add the washed and cut broccoli, diced carrots and potatoes, sauté for a short time, add the chopped onion, fill with water, enough water to cover the vegetables at least 3 finger breadths. Add bouillon, salt, add a little bit of white wine, add the seasoned sage and rosemary.
Heat till it boils and then simmer on a small fire for about 25 minutes.
Season with pepper, if necessary season with sea salt. Purée the soup.

9.10 Carrot and rice gruel soup

Warms the stomach and spleen, harmonizes the intestine, forces Qi, reduces moisture, strengthens spleen and liver, regulates Qi flow, moisturizes, relaxes, builds up Qi, spreads.
Cooking time approx. 10 min
Calories p. portion: 101
1 portion

Quantity of ingredients:
Basic recipe for a rice soup (Congee) 1 cup / 120g. (rec.) - neutral - sweet..... *
Carrot 2 pieces / 100g. (rec.) - neutral - sweet ....earth
Salt 1 teaspoon / 4g. (little) - cold - salty ....water

Cooking instructions:
Peel and grate carrots. Heat the rice soup (according to the basic recipe) till it boils and add the grated carrots and salt. Cook for 10 minutes.

9.11 Carrot drink

Forces spleen, kidney and liver, regulates Qi flow, moisturizes, relaxes, builds up Qi, spreads, moisten the lungs and large intestine, strengthens middle heater, moisturizes.
Cooking time approx. 15 min
Calories p. portion: 143
1 portion
Allergens: H

Quantity of ingredients:
Millet flakes 1 table spoon / 10g. (yes) - cool - sweet, salty........................earth
Carrot 7/8 lbs / 200g. (rec.) - neutral - sweet...earth
Almond puree 1 teaspoon / 3g. (omit) - neutral - sweet ....earth
Honey 1/2 teaspoon / 2g. (little) - cold - sweet ....earth
Water 1/4 cup / 50g. (yes) - cool - salty..earth

Cooking instructions:
Sprinkle millet flakes with 50 ml of cold water and let it swell for 10 minutes.
Juice the fresh carrots or use 200 ml. carrot juice.
Puree the millet flakes, carrot juice, almond paste and honey with the blender.

9.12 Celery juice

Strengthens stomach Qi, moisturizes, relaxes, builds up Qi, spreads.
Cooking time approx. 5 min
Calories p. portion: 33
1 portion
Allergens: L

Quantity of ingredients:
Celery root 1/2 piece / 200g. (rec.) - cool - sweet......................................earth
Water 1 cup / 120g. (yes) - cool - salty..earth
Salt 1 pinch / 0,5g. (little) - cold - salty ....water

Cooking instructions:
Peel celeriac and cut into pieces and juice. Mix with water and salt as needed.

9.13 Chicken soup with egg yolk and parsley

Forces Qi and blood, is very warming, nourishes blood and liver, harmonizes liver and spleen, forces eyesight, preserves the fluids, contracts.
Cooking time approx. 10 min
Calories p. portion: 118
2 portions
Allergens: CL

Quantity of ingredients:
Basic recipe for a chicken soup (warming) 2 cup / 500g. (rec.) - warm - * .... *
Chicken yolk 1 piece / 10g. (little) - neutral - sweet ....earth
Parsley 1 table spoon / 10g. (rec.) - warm - bitter .... wood

Cooking instructions:
Cook the chicken broth according to the basic recipe.
Heat broth and bubble the egg yolk. Sprinkle the chopped parsley over it and let it rest for about 2 minutes. Drink in small sips.

9.14 Corn coffee with cardamom

Dries out, passes downwardly.
Cooking time approx. 5 min
Calories p. portion: 3
1 portion

Quantity of ingredients:
Cereal coffee 1 table spoon / 15g. (yes) - warm - bitter ....fire
Cardamom 2 cores / 1g. (yes) - warm - acrid ....metal
Water 1 cup / 120g. (yes) - cool - salty..earth

Cooking instructions:
Boil water, coffee, sugar and cardamom. Let it set for one min before drinking.

9.15 Cottage cheese with steamed fruit

Moisturizes lungs, cools heat, reduces lung mucus, produces humors, moisturizes, relaxes, builds up Qi, spreads, preserves the fluids, contracts.
Cooking time approx. 20 min
Calories p. portion: 214
2 portions
Allergens: G

Quantity of ingredients:
Cottage cheese 3/4 lbs / 300g. (rec.) - cool - sour .... wood
Apple (sour) 1 piece / 100g. (little) - cool - sour... wood
Pear 1 piece / 100g. (little) - cool - sweet, sour ....earth

Cooking instructions:
Wash apples and pears well, do not peel, and chop small. In a pot with steam filter, boil them al dente, remove and allow to cool down.
Serve the cheese, spread the fruit on it.

9.16 Curdcheesedumplings on strawberry pulp

Preserves the fluids, contracts, moisturizes the lungs, nourishes liver-blood, relaxes.
Cooking time approx. 30 min
Calories p. portion: 553
5 portions
Allergens: ACG

Quantity of ingredients:
Curd cheese 20% 1,1 lbs / 500g. (yes) - cool - sour .... wood
Spelled semolina 3/8 lbs - 6oz / 150g. (yes) - neutral - sweet .... wood
Butter organic 1/8 lbs - 2oz / 40g. (yes) - neutral - sweet...........................earth
Chicken egg 2 pieces / 120g. (little) - neutral - sweet.................................earth
Sugar - icing sugar 2 table spoons / 20g. (little) - cold - sweet ....earth
Salt 1 pinch / 1g. (little) - cold - salty ....water
Breadcrumbs (bread roll) 3 table spoons / 25g. (yes) - cool - sweet, ... wood
Butter organic 1/4 lbs - 4oz / 100g. (yes) - neutral - sweet.........................earth
Strawberries 1,1 lbs / 500g. (yes) - neutral - sweet, sour ....wood
Sugar - icing sugar 3 table spoons / 25g. (little) - cold - sweet ....earth

Cooking instructions:
Curd-cheese, grit, butter, eggs, powdered sugar and salt to a smooth dough. Keep the dough 15 mins in the refrigerator to settle down. Then shape small dumplings with a diameter of approx. 4cm and boil them for

about 10 minutes in slightly boiling salt water. Heat butter in a pan and roast the breadcrumbs golden brown. Roll the dumplings carefully into the crumbs.
Serve the dumplings with the strawberry.

9.17 Fennel and potato gratin

Regulates Qi, warms the inside, lowers cold, forces stomach, relieves constipation, forces Yang, dissolves mucus, reduces wind, spreads. forces Qi, forces spleen, relaxes, builds up Qi, spreads.
Cooking time approx. 1 1/2 hours
Calories p. portion: 147
2 portions
Allergens: CGL

Quantity of ingredients:
Fennel 5/8 oz / 200g. (rec.) - warm - sweet, little acrid...............................earth
Potato 1/4 lbs - 4oz / 125g. (rec.) - neutral - sweet ....earth
Basic recipe for a vegetable soup (nutritious) 1/2 cup / 100g. (rec.) - neutral - **
Butter organic 1 teaspoon / 3g. (yes) - neutral - sweet...............................earth
Rice flour 2 teaspoons / 6g. (yes) - warm - sweet ....metal
Cream sour 10% 1 teaspoon / 3g. (yes) - neutral - sweet ....earth
Salt 1 pinch / 1g. (little) - cold - salty ....water
Sugar cane sugar 1 pinch / 1g. (little) - cool - sweet ....earth
Chicken yolk 1 piece / 10g. (little) - neutral - sweet ....earth
Pepper Cayenne 1 pinch / 0,5g. (omit) - warm - acrid...............................metal
Nutmeg 1 pinch / 0,5g. (yes) - warm - acrid ....metal
Parsley 1 teaspoon / 2g. (rec.) - warm - bitter ....wood
Chives 1 teaspoon / 3g. (omit) - warm - acrid...metal
Butter organic 1 teaspoon / 3g. (yes) - neutral - sweet...............................earth

Cooking instructions:
Cook peeled potatoes and then let cool. Wash the fennel, cut off the stems and remove any outer leaves.
Hold back fennel greens and add it to the sauce with the other herbs later.
Steam the fennel tubers for about 15 - 20 minutes.
Then cut the potatoes and fennel into slices and place in layers in a greased baking dish.
Bring the liquid of fennel broth to the boil and bind it with flour.
Season with sea salt, cayenne pepper, sugar, nutmeg and sour cream. Allow to cool and alloy with egg yolk.
Spread the sauce over the casserole, sprinkle with parmesan and finely chopped parsley and chives. Bake at 200 °C / 392 °F in the oven for half an hour.

9.18 Fennel-Rice Soup

Regulates Qi, warms the inside, lowers cold, forces stomach, relieves constipation, forces Yang, dissolves mucus, reduces wind, spreads, strengthens Qi and kidney Jing, builds up Qi.
Cooking time approx. 15-20 min
Calories p. portion: 156
2 portions
Allergens: EG

Quantity of ingredients:
Basic recipe for a rice soup (Congee) 1 cup / 300g. (rec.) - neutral - sweet..... *
Fennel 1/2 piece / 150g. (rec.) - warm - sweet, little acrid..........................earth
Butter organic 1 table spoon / 15g. (yes) - neutral - sweet..........................earth
Soy sauce 1 dash / 3g. (little) - cold - salty... water

Cooking instructions:
Cook the fennel softly in the rice soup according to the basic recipe.
Before serving, add a piece of butter and some soy sauce.

9.19 Figs with mozzarella and honey

Moisturizes the lungs and large intestine, reduces mucusfire, passes downwardly, strengthens middle heater, reduces internal heat, dissolves stagnation.
Cooking time approx. 10 min
Calories p. portion: 415
1 portion
Allergens: GO

Quantity of ingredients:
Fig 4 pieces / 100g. (yes) - warm - sweet...earth
Mozzarella 1 piece / 50g. (little) - neutral - sweet ....earth
Basil (fresh) 1/2 bunch / 50g. (yes) - warm - acrid, bitter...........................metal
Honey 2 table spoons / 24g. (little) - cold - sweet.......................................earth
Pepper (ground) 1 pinch / 0,1g. () - warm - acrid ....metal
Grapeseed oil 1 table spoon / 12g. (little) - cool - sweet ....earth
Vinegar Balsamico white 1 table spoon / 12g. (little) - warm - sour, bitter. wood

Cooking instructions:
Quarter fresh figs, dice buffalo mozzarella, pluck basil leaves.
Mix a dressing with light balsamic vinegar, grapeseed oil and honey and season to taste.
Place the figs on the edge of the appropriate plate. Spread the mozzarella cubes and season with black pepper. Spread whole or

roughly sliced basil leaves over it and moisten with the marinade. Spiced pizza bread goes perfectly with it.

9.20 Fine Russian borscht

Forces spleen and stomach Qi, nourishes blood, strengthens stomach Qi, builds up Qi, spreads, strengthens spleen and liver, regulates Qi flow, moisturizes, relaxes.
Cooking time approx. 30 min
Calories p. portion: 172
6 portions
Allergens: AGLO

Quantity of ingredients:
Red beet 5/8 oz / 200g. (rec.) - neutral - bitter ....earth
Sunflower oil 1 table spoon / 10g. (little) - cool - sweet ....earth
Onion (shallot) 2 pieces / 40g. (omit) - warm - acrid, sweet ....metal
Carrot 2 pieces / 140g. (rec.) - neutral - sweet...earth
Celery root 1 piece / 500g. (rec.) - cool - sweet..earth
Parsley root 1 piece / 150g. (rec.) - cool - sweet ....earth
Leek 1/8 lbs - 2oz / 50g. (omit) - warm - acrid ....metal
Basic recipe for a vegetable soup (nutritious) 3 cups / 650g. (rec.) - neutral - **
Bay leaf 1 Leaf / 0,2g. (yes) - warm - acrid..metal
Juniper berry 2 pieces / 2g. (yes) - warm - sweet, acrid, bitter ....fire
Nutmeg 1 pinch / 1g. (yes) - warm - acrid ....metal
Savoy cabbage / kale 5/8 oz / 200g. (omit) - neutral - sweet......................earth
Salt 1 pinch / 1g. (little) - cold - salty ....water
Pepper (ground) 1 pinch / 0,5g. () - warm - acrid ....metal
Ground 1 pinch / 1g. (rec.) - warm - acrid..metal
Red wine 1/2 cup / 125g. (omit) - warm - bitter ....fire
Sour cream 15% fat 1 table spoon / 10g. (yes) - cool - sour ....wood
Dill 1 teaspoon / 10g. (rec.) - warm - acrid ....metal
White bread (wheat bread) 6 slices / 120g. (yes) - cool - sweet................wood

Cooking instructions:
Fry some beetroot in oil. Fry the onions, carrots, celery, parsley root and leek well in another pan. Add the stock and the wine; then add bay leaves, juniper berries and nutmeg and simmer for 15 minutes. Remove the bay leaf and puree everything.
Heat more broth separately, simmer the steamed beetroot in it. Add cabbage or white cabbage after half the cooking time and let it steep. At the end, add the pureed vegetables and season with salt, pepper, ground cumin and a little red wine. Garnish with some sour cream and finely chopped dill in the plate. Serve with a slice of white bread.

9.21 Fish soup with rosemary

Strengthens kidney Qi, strengthens blood and fluids, promotes urination, regulates Qi, dries out, passes downwardly, strengthens spleen and liver, regulates Qi flow, moisturizes, relaxes, builds up Qi.
Cooking time approx. 30 min
Calories p. portion: 271
4 portions
Allergens: DLO

Quantity of ingredients:
Basic recipe for a fish soup 2 cup / 500g. (rec.) - cool - * .... *
Rosemary 1/2 bunch / 7g. (yes) - warm - bitter .... fire
Onion (spring onion) 1 piece / 20g. (omit) - warm - acrid .... metal
Olive oil 2 table spoons / 35g. (little) - cool - sweet .... earth
Fish pieces mixed 5/8 lbs - 8oz / 250g. (yes) - warm - sweet, salty .... water
Carrot 1 piece / 120g. (rec.) - neutral - sweet .... earth
Parsnip 1 piece / 180g. (yes) - cool - bitter .... fire
Celery root 1 slice / 20g. (rec.) - cool - sweet .... earth
Salt 1 pinch / 1g. (little) - cold - salty .... water
Peppercorns 2 pieces / 1g. (omit) - warm - acrid .... metal
Garlic 1 clove / 3g. (omit) - hot - acrid .... metal

Cooking instructions:
Fry the onion and garlic in oil. Add fish broth. Add diced carrots, parsnips and celery. Season with salt and peppercorns. Simmer the soup on a low heat for 25 minutes.
Wash the fish, drizzle with lemon juice, divide into pieces and add to the soup with the pink rosemary. Cook for 5 min on low heat.
Add the chives and parsley and season the soup with the salt.

9.22 Frozen pineapple juice

Nourishes fluids, diuretic, relieves inflammation, supports the urination, cleanses the skin, preserves the fluids, contracts.
Cooking time approx. 1 1/2 hours
Calories p. portion: 29
1 portion

Quantity of ingredients:
Pineapple 1/8 lbs - 2oz / 50g. (little) - cold - sweet, sour .... wood

Cooking instructions:
Juice pineapple yourself or freeze the organic pineapple juice in small portions and if necessary suck.

9.23 Hot water with grape juice

Juice or blood deficiency
Cooking time approx. 5 min
Calories p. portion: 87
1 portion

Quantity of ingredients:
Grape juice red 1 cup / 120g. (little) - neutral - sweet, sour.........................earth
Water 1/2 cup / 60g. (yes) - cool - salty...earth

Cooking instructions:
Heat the water till it boils and add it to the grape juice.

9.24 Kohlrabi Potatoes mash

Moves Qi and blood, reduces moisture, forces Qi, forces spleen, relieves inflammation, moisturizes, relaxes, builds up Qi, spreads, forces kidney Jing.
Cooking time approx. 25 min
Calories p. portion: 278
1 portion
Allergens: CG

Quantity of ingredients:
Kohlrabi 1/2 piece / 150g. (yes) - neutral - acrid, sweet ....earth
Potato 1/4 lbs - 4oz / 100g. (rec.) - neutral - sweet ....earth
Butter organic 1 table spoon / 10g. (yes) - neutral - sweet..........................earth
Chicken yolk 1 piece / 25g. (little) - neutral - sweet ....earth

Cooking instructions:
Remove the kohlrabi leaves, wash the tuber and tender leaves and the potatoes thoroughly. Peel the kohlrabi and potatoes, cut into cubes about 1 cm in size. Melt half the butter in a small saucepan, add the kohlrabi and the potatoes and fry in it. Steam with 2 tablespoons of water in a closed saucepan over low heat for about 15 minutes. Meanwhile, free the tenderest kohlrabi leaves from the stems and chop very finely. In total, at most 2 tablespoons of leaf pieces should be used. Add this to the vegetables about 5 minutes before the end of the cooking time. Stir in the egg yolk and bring to the boil again. Put the vegetables in a plate and mix with the remaining butter and egg yolk. (Crush for the baby with a fork.)

9.25 Mango banana yoghurt drink ice cold

Reduces internal heat, moisturizes intestines, moisturizes, relaxes, builds up Qi, spreads, moisturizes dryness, preserves the fluids, contracts.
Cooking time approx. 5 min
Calories p. portion: 121
2 portions
Allergens: G

Quantity of ingredients:
Mango juice 1/2 cup / 100g. (little) - cold - sweet, sour .... wood
Yogurt (natural, 1.5% fat) 1/4 lbs - 4oz / 100g. (yes) - cool - sour .... wood
Banana 1/2 piece / 150g. (rec.) - cool - sweet, rough................................earth
Acerola fruit nectar or powder 1 teaspoon / 2g. (little) - warm - sour......... wood

Cooking instructions:
Mix all the ingredients and 2-3 ice cubes in a blender.

9.26 Mashed banana

Reduces internal heat, regulates gastrointestinal function, moisturizes intestines, relaxes, builds Qi, spreads.
Cooking time approx. 7 min
Calories p. portion: 144
1 portion

Quantity of ingredients:
Banana 1 piece / 150g. (rec.) - cool - sweet, rough....................................earth

Cooking instructions:
Mix the banana with the fork or purée with a blender. Leave to brown for at least 5 minutes.

9.27 Melanzani with olive oil and turmeric

Cools and moves blood, reduces external and internal wind, reduces internal heat, nourishes liver-Yin, cools heat, produces humors, moisturizes, relaxes, builds up Qi, spreads.
Cooking time approx. 30 min
Calories p. portion: 432
2 portions
Allergens: A

Quantity of ingredients:
Aubergine 2 pieces / 300g. (yes) - cool - sweet ....earth
Olive oil 4 table spoons / 60g. (little) - cool - sweet ....earth
Tomato 4 pieces / 200g. (little) - cold - sweet-sour.................................... wood
Turmeric (yellow root) 1/2 teaspoon / 1g. (yes) - warm - bitter........................ *
Ground 1 pinch / 1g. (rec.) - warm - acrid.. metal
Salt 1 pinch / 1g. (little) - cold - salty .... water
White bread (wheat bread) 4 slices / 80g. (yes) - cool - sweet.................. wood

Cooking instructions:
Cut the Melanzani into slices and spread them with the tomatoes on a baking tray. Sprinkle with olive oil and then with turmeric, caraway and salt. Bake them in the tube 20 min.
Serve with the white bread.

9.28 Nettle-chard soup

Drains moisture down, strengthens blood, cools liver heat.
Cooking time approx. 30 min
Calories p. portion: 52
4 portions

Quantity of ingredients:
Nettles 1 handful / 10g. (yes) - neutral - bitter .... wood
Chard 1 lbs / 500g. (yes) - cool - bitter, sweet..earth
Salt 1 pinch / 1g. (little) - cold - salty .... water
Water 2 cup / 400g. (yes) - cool - salty...earth
Olive oil 1 table spoon / 10g. (little) - cool - sweet ....earth
Pepper (ground) 1 pinch / 0,5g. () - warm - acrid .... metal

Cooking instructions:
Heat the oil in a saucepan, add the washed and finely chopped Swiss chard. Salt and let simmer for 10 minutes. Add the chopped nettles and cook for another 10 minutes. Add pepper and puree.

9.29 Olive oil with lemon juice

Moisturizes, relaxes, builds up Qi, spreads, cools heat, preserves the fluids, contracts.
Cooking time approx. 1 min
Calories p. portion: 93
1 portion

Quantity of ingredients:
Olive oil 1 table spoon / 10g. (little) - cool - sweet ....earth
Lemon juice 1 teaspoon / 4g. (omit) - cold - sour .... wood

Cooking instructions:
In case of acute constipation take 1 tablespoon of olive oil with lemon juice in the morning on an empty stomach.

9.30 Pear compote

Moisturizes lungs, reduces lung mucus, nourishes lungs Qi.
Cooking time approx. 20 min
Calories p. portion: 100
3 portions

Quantity of ingredients:
Water 1 1/2 cups / 240g. (yes) - cool - salty ....earth
Pear 4 pieces / 500g. (little) - cool - sweet, sour ....earth

Cooking instructions:
Halve organic pears. Cores and skin can be used. Pear in the pot and add water. Simmer for up to 20 minutes until pears are tender.

9.31 Potato pancakes

Forces Qi, forces spleen, relieves inflammation, moisturizes, relaxes, builds up Qi, spreads, forces blood, Yin and Jing, nourishes Yin, Moisturizes in case of internal dryness, forces blood, forces spleen, calms nerves and stomach.
Cooking time approx. 15 min
Calories p. portion: 893
1 portion
Allergens: ACG

Quantity of ingredients:
Potato (mealy) 5/8 lbs - 8oz / 250g. (rec.) - neutral - sweet.......................earth
Wheat flour 1/2 oz / 10g. (yes) - cool - sweet, salty.................................... wood
Chicken egg 1 piece / 35g. (little) - neutral - sweet ....earth
Rapeseed oil 2 table spoons / 20g. (little) - neutral - sweet......................earth
Salt 1 pinch / 1g. (little) - cold - salty .... water
Cream sour 20% 1/8 lbs - 2oz / 50g. (little) - neutral - sweet....................earth
Salt 1 pinch / 1g. (little) - cold - salty .... water

Cooking instructions:
Grater the peeled potatoes finely, add the remaining ingredients, mix well and salt. Heat the oil and add small flat cakes to the pan with the spoon. Roast the potato pancakes on both sides crispy golden brown. Place them on the
plate with sour cream, salt and sprinkle with herbs.

9.32 Potato-basil soup

Strengthens stomach Qi, moisturizes, relaxes, builds up Qi, spreads, forces Qi, forces spleen, relieves inflammation, spreads, strengthens spleen and liver, regulates Qi flow.
Cooking time approx. 25 min
Calories p. portion: 96
4 portions
Allergens: L

Quantity of ingredients:
Water 2 cups / 450g. (yes) - cool - salty ....earth
Potato 4 pieces / 200g. (rec.) - neutral - sweet...earth
Carrot 2 pieces / 100g. (rec.) - neutral - sweet ....earth
Celery root 1 piece / 500g. (rec.) - cool - sweet...earth
Pepper (ground) 1 pinch / 0,5g. () - warm - acrid ....metal
Ground 1 pinch / 1g. (rec.) - warm - acrid...metal
Garlic 1 clove / 3g. (omit) - hot - acrid ....metal
Salt 1 pinch / 1g. (little) - cold - salty ....water
Lemon 1 teaspoon / 3g. (omit) - cold - sour..wood
Basil (fresh) 1 Bunch / 50g. (yes) - warm - acrid, bitter ....metal
Sugar cane sugar 1 pinch / 1g. (little) - cool - sweet ....earth
Olive oil 1 table spoon / 10g. (little) - cool - sweet ....earth

Cooking instructions:
Peeled and chopped 4 medium potatoes in a pot of hot water and 2 chopped medium carrots, a piece of celery root, a pinch of pepper, a pinch of ground cumin, crushed a small clove of garlic, a pinch of salt, 1 teaspoon of lemon juice, simmer until the Vegetables is soft.

Add 1 bunch finely chopped basil into one half of the soup and puree everything; stir in the other half of the basil; with rose paprika, a pinch of whole cane sugar, 1 tablespoon of olive oil or butter, freshly ground pepper, salt to taste.

9.33 Pumpkin soup

Forces lungs and spleen, diuretic, forces Qi, protects liver, forces Qi, forces spleen, relieves inflammation, moisturizes, relaxes, builds up Qi, spreads, strengthens spleen and liver, regulates Qi flow, moisturizes, relaxes, builds up Qi, spreads.
Cooking time approx. 1 hour
Calories p. portion: 105
3 portions

Quantity of ingredients:
Pumpkin 3/4 lbs / 300g. (rec.) - warm - sweet.................................earth
Carrot 2 pieces / 100g. (rec.) - neutral - sweet.............................earth
Potato 2 pieces / 120g. (rec.) - neutral - sweet............................earth
Olive oil 1 table spoon / 10g. (little) - cool - sweet.....................earth
Onion white 1 piece / 50g. (omit) - warm - acrid.........................metal
Water 1 cup / 120g. (yes) - cool - salty......................................earth
Parsley 1 table spoon / 7g. (rec.) - warm - bitter.......................wood
Anise (Common Fennel) 1 pinch / 1g. (rec.) - warm - acrid.......earth
Salt 1 pinch / 1g. (little) - cold - salty.......................................water

Cooking instructions:
Add the olive oil to the pan, add the diced pumpkin, diced carrots and potatoes. Roast them shortly, add the finely chopped onion, fill with water, add enough water to cover the vegetables at least 3 finger-widths. Boil at low heat.

Season with sea salt, add small cutted parsley, a pinch of anise (little). Allow to simmer for about 35 minutes. Then purée the soup and add some water, depending on the consistency of
the soup.

9.34 Quick zucchini soup

Reduces mucus, preserves the fluids, cools liver fire, forces stomach Qi.
Cooking time approx. 10 min
Calories p. portion: 42
4 portions

Quantity of ingredients:
Zucchini 2-3 pieces / 500g. (rec.) - cool - sweet.........................earth
Onion white 1 piece / 50g. (omit) - warm - acrid.........................metal
Corn germ oil 2 table spoons / 6g. (little) - neutral - sweet.........earth
Parsley 1 table spoon / 7g. (rec.) - warm - bitter.......................wood

Chives 1 teaspoon / 3g. (omit) - warm - acrid...metal
Water 2 cup / 400g. (yes) - cool - salty...earth

Cooking instructions:
Fry chopped onion in oil. Add sliced zucchini and sauté well. Pour with water. Chop parsley and chives, add and puree everything.

9.35 Rhubarb and apple jelly

Moisturizes, relaxes, builds up Qi, spreads, cools heat, preserves the fluids, contracts, strengthens middle heater, moisturizes, cools heat, distributes mucus, derives wind-cold and wind-heat, brings the stomach Qi in motion, solves congestion.
Cooking time approx. 15 min
Calories p. portion: 180
2 portions

Quantity of ingredients:
Rhubarb 5/8 oz / 200g. (yes) - cold - sour.. wood
Apple juice (natural cloudy) 1 cup / 300g. (little) - cool - sweet ....earth
Corn starch 1 oz / 30g. (yes) - neutral - sweet ....earth
Honey 1/2 oz / 20g. (little) - cold - sweet ....earth
Vanilla sugar natural 1 pinch / 0,5g. (little) - neutral - sweet.............................. *
Cinnamon ground 1 pinch / 0,5g. (yes) - hot - acrid, sweet.............................. *
Peppermint 2 leaves / 2g. (yes) - cool - acrid, bitter ....metal

Cooking instructions:
Add the cornstarch to a 1/2 cup apple juice.
Simmer the rhubarb in 1 cup of water for 10 min.
Add the remaining apple juice and the cornstarch, stir, heat till it boils again.
Sweet with honey and season with vanilla and cinnamon. Spread the mixture on dessert bowls and garnish with mint.

9.36 Rice congee with carrots and fennel

Nutritious builds up Qi, forces the digestive functions.
Cooking time approx. 2 hours and more
Calories p. portion: 131
3 portions
Allergens: G

Quantity of ingredients:
Basic recipe for a rice soup (Congee) 2 cup / 500g. (rec.) - neutral - sweet..... *
Carrot 2 pieces / 100g. (rec.) - neutral - sweet...earth
Fennel 1 piece / 250g. (rec.) - warm - sweet, little acrid.............................earth
Butter organic 1 teaspoon / 3g. (yes) - neutral - sweet..............................earth
Cardamom 1/2 teaspoon / 1g. (yes) - warm - acrid...................................metal

Cooking instructions:
Cook rice congee according to basic recipe.
Clean and cut carrots and fennel.

When carrots and fennel are cooked from the beginning, they serve
wholesomeness. If added shortly before the end of the cooking time,
taste and vitamins are retained.

Refine with butter and cardamom before serving.

9.37 Rice with parsnips

Regulates Qi, dries out, passes downwardly, warms the stomach and
spleen, harmonizes the intestine, forces Qi, reduces moisture.
moisturizes, relaxes, builds up Qi, spreads. distributes mucus, activates
Wei Qi, forces Qi.
Cooking time approx. 45 min
Calories p. portion: 206
3 portions

Quantity of ingredients:
Rice variety any 1 cup / 120g. (yes) - warm - sweet................................. metal
Water 1 1/2 cups / 200g. (yes) - cool - salty...earth
Salt 1 pinch / 1g. (little) - cold - salty .... water
Parsnip 3-4 pieces / 450g. (yes) - cool - bitter...fire
Olive oil 1 table spoon / 10g. (little) - cool - sweet....................................earth
Sage 1 teaspoon / 3g. (yes) - cool - bitter, spicy ....fire

Cooking instructions:
Peel the parsnips and cut into slices. Fry for a short time in oil. Add the
rice and fry again for a short time. Add the water and cook it at least 30
min. Sprinkle with fresh chopped sage.

9.38 Rosemary Potatoes

Forces Qi, forces spleen, relieves inflammation, relaxes, builds up Qi, spreads.
Cooking time approx. 30 min
Calories p. portion: 188
2 portions

Quantity of ingredients:
Potato 6-8 pieces / 420g. (rec.) - neutral - sweet ....earth
Olive oil 1 table spoon / 10g. (little) - cool - sweet ....earth
Rosemary 1 teaspoon / 2g. (yes) - warm - bitter ....fire

Cooking instructions:
Cut the potatoes into half´s, apply a little olive oil on the cut surface, then salt, sprinkle 2 - 3 rosemary needles on the potatoes.
Place the potatoes on the baking tray and bake them in the preheated oven for approx. 25 minutes to 190°C/374°F.

9.39 Semolina porridge with banana

Nourishes fluids, moisturizes dryness, produces humors, moisturizes intestines, cools inner heat, preserves the
fluids.
Cooking time approx. 15 min
Calories p. portion: 307
1 portion
Allergens: AG

Quantity of ingredients:
Cow's milk (3.5% fat) 3/4 cup - 6 oz / 200g. (little) - neutral - sweet...........earth
Spelled semolina 3 table spoons / 30g. (yes) - neutral - sweet .... wood
Butter organic 1 teaspoon / 4g. (yes) - neutral - sweet..............................earth
Banana 1/2 piece / 50g. (rec.) - cool - sweet, rough....................................earth

Cooking instructions:
Heat the half of the milk in a small pot. Add the semolina and boil it shortly in the milk. Let it swell at low heat for 3 minutes with constant stirring. Remove the pot from the heat, add the remaining milk with the snow bean and place the mush in a small bowl. Add the butter and the battered banana.
For adults, a pinch of cinnamon can be spread over it.

9.40 Spring vegetables

Cools heat, diuretic, cools blood, reduces mucus, moisturizes, relaxes, builds Qi, distributes, strengthen the middle, nourishes lung Yin, produces humors.
Cooking time approx. 1 1/2 hour
Calories p. portion: 64
8 portions
Allergens: G

Quantity of ingredients:
Carrot 1,1 lbs / 500g. (rec.) - neutral - sweet..earth
Kohlrabi 1,1 lbs / 500g. (yes) - neutral - acrid, sweet ....earth
Butter organic 2 table spoons / 20g. (yes) - neutral - sweet ....earth
Water 1/2 cup / 125g. (yes) - cool - salty...earth

Cooking instructions:
Wash the vegetables thoroughly. Clean and peel carrots and turnip cabbage. From the turnip cabbage, finely chop some delicate leaves and set aside. Rasp the carrots and the turnip cabbage. Melt the butter, add the water and the vegetables and cook over medium heat for about 30 minutes. Stir occasionally. Spread the vegetables and cooked water to about 8 deep-frozen bags to a100-150 g (depending on the age of the child). Close the bags, allow them to cool down and freeze them for max 3 months.
If necessary thaw, boil and mix with 80g of boiled potatoes and an egg.
(The recipe can easily be varied if you want to use cauliflower, peas or zucchini)

9.41 Tea from anise

Warms the middle, forces stomach and spleen, warms stomach, reduces cold-evil, harmonizes stomach-Qi, warms kidney.
Cooking time approx. 15 min
Calories p. portion: 3
4 portions

Quantity of ingredients:
Anise (Common Fennel) 1 teaspoon / 3g. (rec.) - warm - acrid..................earth
Water 2 cup / 500g. (yes) - cool - salty..earth

Cooking instructions:
Heat the water till it boils and put it aside. Add anise.
10 min. to let go.
Pour through a tea strainer. Sweet to taste with honey.

In order to achieve a salutary effect, you should drink 2 cups of anise tea per day.

9.42 Tea from coriander

Sudorific, reduces wind.
Cooking time approx. 10 min
Calories p. portion: 2
4 portions

Quantity of ingredients:
Coriander 1 teaspoon / 3g. (yes) - warm - acrid .... metal
Water 2 cup / 500g. (yes) - cool - salty .... earth

Cooking instructions:
Heat the water till it boils and put it aside. Add coriander and 10 min. to let go. Sweet to taste with honey. Strain when pouring.

9.43 Tea from elderberry blossom tea

Derives wind-cold and wind-heat.
Cooking time approx. 10 min
Calories p. portion: 7
4 portions
Allergens.
Quantity of ingredients:
Water 2 cup / 500g. (yes) - cool - salty .... earth
Elderberry blossom tea 1 teaspoon / 3g. (yes) .... *

Cooking instructions:
Heat the water till it boils and put it aside. Add elderberry blossom tea and 10 min. to let go. Sweet to taste with honey. Strain when pouring.

9.44 Tea from ground

Reduces mucus and moist heat in the liver and gallbladder, against liver
Qi stagnation, spleen qi deficiency, spleen and kidney Yang-deficit.
Cooking time approx. 10 min
Calories p. portion: 2
4 portions

Quantity of ingredients:
Ground 1 teaspoon / 3g. (rec.) - warm - acrid .... metal
Water 2 cup / 500g. (yes) - cool - salty...earth

Cooking instructions:
Heat the water till it boils and put it aside. Add crushed cumin and leave
for 10 min. to let go. Sweet to taste with honey. Strain when pouring.

Drink 1 cup 2 times a day.

9.45 Tea from marjoram

Dissolves stagnation, directs upwards.
Cooking time approx. 10 min
Calories p. portion: 0
4 portions

Quantity of ingredients:
Marjoram 2 teaspoons / 6g. (yes) - warm - bitter....................................... metal
Water 2 cup / 500g. (yes) - cool - salty...earth

Cooking instructions:
Heat the water till it boils and put it aside. Add marjoram and 10 min. to
let go. Sweet to taste with honey. Strain when pouring.

9.46 Tender fennel vegetables

Regulates Qi, warms the inside, lowers cold, forces stomach, relieves
constipation, forces Yang, dissolves mucus, reduces wind, spreads.
Cooking time approx. 25 min
Calories p. portion: 70
2 portions
Allergens: G

Quantity of ingredients:

Potato 1 piece / 50g. (rec.) - neutral - sweet ....earth
Fennel 1/4 lbs - 4oz / 100g. (rec.) - warm - sweet, little acrid ....earth
Water 2 table spoons / 20g. (yes) - cool - salty ....earth
Butter organic 1 table spoon / 10g. (yes) - neutral - sweet..........................earth

Cooking instructions:

Wash the potato and peel with a peeler. Cut into cubes of about 2 cm.
Wash the fennel, remove stained, dark spots and cut the tuber. Heat till
it boils with 2 tablespoons of water in a small saucepan. Cook on low
heat for about 15 minutes. Fish out the caraway seeds. Puree the
vegetables with the blender and stir in the butter.
Fennel and caraway soothe the stomach and prevent bloating. In
addition, fennel contains a lot of vitamin C and folic acid. An ideal meal
for sick children.

9.47 Tomato with mozzarella

Nourishes liver-Yin, cools heat, produces humors.
Cooking time approx. 5 min
Calories p. portion: 436
1 portion
Allergens: AG

Quantity of ingredients:

Mozzarella 1 piece / 50g. (little) - neutral - sweet ....earth
Tomato 2 pieces / 100g. (little) - cold - sweet-sour....................................wood
Salt 1 pinch / 1g. (little) - cold - salty ....water
Basil (fresh) 5 leaves / 6g. (yes) - warm - acrid, bitter ....metal
Olive oil 2 table spoons / 20g. (little) - cool - sweet ....earth
White bread (wheat bread) 2 slices / 40g. (yes) - cool - sweet..................wood

Cooking instructions:

Cut tomatoes and mozzarella into slices. Serve with salt, basil and olive
oil. Serve with white bread.

9.48 Vanilla pudding

Nourishes fluids, moisturizes dryness, produces humors, moisturizes
intestines, cools inner heat.
Cooking time approx. 10 min
Calories p. portion: 254
2 portions
Allergens: G

Quantity of ingredients:
Cow's milk (3.5% fat) 2 cups / 500g. (little) - neutral - sweet......................earth
Sugar white 1 table spoon / 12g. (little) - cold - sweet...............................earth
Pudding powder vanilla 1 package.. *

Cooking instructions:
Give 3-5 tablespoons of milk into a cup, bring the rest in a pot to boil.
Pour the powdered pudding into the cup and stir until free of lumpy. As
soon as the milk boils, add the mixture and simmer under low heat for
about 3 minutes. Divide into prepared bowls.

9.49 Vegetable porridge

Strengthens spleen and liver, regulates Qi flow, moisturizes, relaxes,
builds up Qi, distributes, relieves inflammation, strengthens Qi, blood
and Jing and middle heat, strengthens essence, preserves the fluids,
pulls together.
Cooking time approx. 20 min
Calories p. portion: 161
1 portion
Allergens: G

Quantity of ingredients:
Potato 1 piece / 50g. (rec.) - neutral - sweet ....earth
Carrot (Early Carrot) 1/4 lbs - 4oz / 100g. (rec.) - neutral - sweet ....earth
Chicken meat 1 oz / 30g. (little) - warm - sweet .... wood
Butter organic 1 table spoon / 10g. (yes) - neutral - sweet.........................earth

Cooking instructions:
Wash the potato and put it unpeeled in a small pot. Cover with a little
water and bring to boil, then cook the potatoes
on a low heat for 15-20 minutes.
Meanwhile, wash the carrots, clean, peel and cut into pieces about 2
cm in size. Steam with 3 tablespoons of water and the meat in a pot for
about 15 minutes.
Finely chop the carrots and meat with a blender. Add the butter and
puree everything.

9.50 Vegetable semolina soup

Strengthens spleen and liver, regulates Qi flow, builds up Qi, dries out, passes downwardly, reduces moisture, regulates Qi.
Cooking time approx. 20 min
Calories p. portion: 199
3 portions
Allergens: AEGL

Quantity of ingredients:
Basic recipe for a vegetable soup (nutritious) 2 cup / 500g. (rec.) - neutral - *. *
Potato 1 piece / 80g. (rec.) - neutral - sweet ....earth
Parsnip 1 piece / 180g. (yes) - cool - bitter..fire
Carrot 1 piece / 120g. (rec.) - neutral - sweet...earth
Celery root 3/8 lbs - 6oz / 150g. (rec.) - cool - sweet..................................earth
Kohlrabi 1/2 piece / 200g. (yes) - neutral - acrid, sweet ....earth
Beans (green, fresh) 1/4 lbs / 100g. (omit) - neutral - sweet ....water
Wheat semolina 2 table spoons / 24g. (yes) - cool - sweet, salty.............. wood
Lovage 1/2 teaspoon / 2g. (rec.) - warm - acrid, bitter.............................. metal
Butter organic 1 table spoon / 20g. (yes) - neutral - sweet.........................earth
Soy sauce 1 teaspoon / 3g. (little) - cold - salty..water

Cooking instructions:
Worm the prepared vegetable soup; cook the vegetables in the soup softly. Spread some wheatgrass and let it swell. At the end, add lovage-green and a little butter and taste with soy sauce.

9.51 Warming carrot soup

Forces Qi und warms Yang.
Cooking time approx. 30 min
Calories p. portion: 133
3 portions
Allergens: HL

Quantity of ingredients:
Carrot 4 pieces / 250g. (rec.) - neutral - sweet ....earth
Walnut oil 2 table spoons / 20g. (little) - neutral - sweet............................earth
Onion (shallot) 2 pieces / 40g. (omit) - warm - acrid, sweet ....metal
Anise (Common Fennel) 1/2 teaspoon / 1g. (rec.) - warm - acrid...............earth
Nutmeg 1 pinch / 1g. (yes) - warm - acrid ....metal
Ginger fresh 1/2 teaspoon / 1g. (omit) - warm - acrid...............................metal
Salt 1 pinch / 1g. (little) - cold - salty ....water
Basic recipe for a vegetable soup (nutritious) 2 cup / 500g. (rec.) - neutral - *. *
Parsley 1 table spoon / 10g. (rec.) - warm - bitter .... wood

Cooking instructions:
Heat walnut oil in a hot pot and fry onions; steam the carrots in it; add anise, nutmeg, a little ginger, salt and sauté everything; add water or vegetable- or meat stock; cook everything soft and then puree; fold in parsley at the end.

Recommendation: Suitable for the cold season, especially if you use meat broth as a liquid for infusion.

10 Effects of food

10.1 Use ingredients: recommendable

Aloe juice
Anise (Common Fennel)
Asparagus (green or white)
Banana
Banana (cooking banana)
Black caraway
Blackberry´s
Blue mallow tee
Cantaloupe
Carrot
Carrot (Early Carrot)
Carrot juice without sugar
Celery root
Chamomile
Chervil
Chervil dried
Cottage cheese
Cress
Crucian
Dill
Elderberries
Elderberry blossom tee

Fennel
Fennel seeds ground
Fennel tea
Gourd
Ground
Ground caraway
Herbal tea mix
Hokkaido pumpkin
Lamb's lettuce
Lovage
Parsley
Parsley root
Potato
Potato (mealy)
Pumpkin
Red beet
Spinach
Turnips
Watermelon
Wax gourd
Zucchini

10.2 Use ingredients: yes

Amaranth
Amaranth Pops
Angelica root
Apple puree
Arrowroot
Artichoke
Aubergine
Baking powder
Balm
Bamboo shoots
Banchatee (green tea)
barberry
Barley
Barley flour
Barley grass powder
Barley grouts
Barley malt
Barley not peeled
Basil
Basil (fresh)
Batavia
Bay leaf
Berries of the season
Bitter Herb liqueur

Blackberry leaves
Blueberry
Borage
Boxhorn clover seeds
Bread roll
Bread with carob kernel flour
Breadcrumbs (wheat bread, bread roll)
Broccoli
Buckbean
Buckwheat
Buckwheat (roasted) Kasha
Bulgur (cereals)
Burdock root tea
Butter (half fat)
Butter organic
Buttermilk
Calamari
Carambola (Star fruit)
Cardamom
Carob flour, St. john's bread
Celery sticks
Cereal coffee
Channa-Dal
Chard

Chicken egg white
Chickweed
Chicory
Chlorella (fresh water)
Chrysanthemum blossom tea
Cinnamon ground
Cinnamon sticks
Clove
Cod
Codfish
Coix (seeds) YiYi Ren
Compote (fruits of the season)
Coriander
Coriander (fresh)
Corn
Corn (fast polenta)
Corn (roasted)
Corn flour
Corn Grease (Polenta)
Corn silk tea
Corn starch
Couscous
Cow's milk (1.5% fat)
Crab
Cranberry
Cranberry
Cranberry jam
Cranberry juice
Cream 10% coffee cream
Cream sour 10%
Creamer
Crispbread
Cumin (Caraway seed)
Curd cheese 20%
Currant (black)
Currant (red)
Currant (white)
Daisy
Dandelion (young plants)
Dandelion juice
Dandelionroots tea
Dashi
Dulse (seaweed)
Endive salad
Fenugreek (Trigonella foenum-
graecum)
Feta cheese
Fig
Fish pieces mixed (fresh water)
Flounder
Flower pollen
Freshwater crab
Freshwater fish
Fruit tea

Galangal
Gelatin white
Gelee Royal
Gentian root
Ginkgo fruit
Ginseng root
Goat and sheep's milk
Goat cheese
Gooseberry
Green tea
Guava
Halibut (Flatfish)
Hawthorn
Herbs bitter
Herbs different varieties
Herbs of Provence
Herbs various
Herbs wild
Hibiscus tea
Hijiki
Hyssop
Iceberg lettuce
Jasmine blossoms tee
Jellyfish
Juniper berry
Kalmus
Kefir
King Solomon's-seal
Kohlrabi
Kukicha tea
Kumquats
Ladyfingers
Lady's mantle
Lamb's lettuce
Lavender blossoms
Leaf salads (bitter)
Lemon Balm (dried)
Lemon Balm (fresh)
Lemongrass
Lettuce
Licorice root tea
Lime blossom tea
Liver smoothing tea
Lobster
Longane
Lovage seeds
Luo Han Guo fruit
Lychee
Lychee in Preserved
Lye roll
Mallow (Malva sylvestris) blossom tea
Mare's milk
Marjoram
Mediterranean fish (cod, plaice,

haddock, sea eel, mackerel)
Medlar
Millet
Millet flakes
Mineral water
Miso
Miso black (fermented)
Mulberry fruit
Mulled Wine Spice
Mullet
Mussels
Nasturtium (nose-twister or nose-tweaker)
Nettles
Noodles (wheat) with egg
Noodles (wheat, lasagne) with egg
Noodles (wheat, ribbon noodles) with egg
Noodles (wheat, spaghetti) with egg
Nori, purple seaweed, red algae
Nutmeg
Oat
Oat flour
Oat fusion (baby food)
Oat milk
Octopus
Octopus
Okra
Orange blossom
Oregano dried
Oregano fresh
Oysters
Papaya
Parsnip
Passion blossoms tea
Passion fruit
Pearl barley
Pearl barley
Peppermint
Peppermint tea
Perch
Pimento
Plaice
Pomegranate
Potato flour
Prickly pear
Processed cheese 12%
Pudding powder vanilla
Quince
Quinoa
Radicchio
Radish black
Radish leaves
Raspberry

Raspberry leaf tea
Red berry (without sugar)
Rhubarb
Ribworttea
Rice (fragrance)
Rice (Gaoliang / Sorghum)
Rice Basmati
Rice flour
Rice long grain rice
Rice malt
Rice mash
Rice noodles
Rice red
Rice round grain
Rice starch
Rice sticky
Rice sweet
Rice variety any
Romaine lettuce / lettuce salad
Rose blossom tea
Rose hip
Rose hip tea
Rose leaf tea
Rosefish
Rosemary
Rusk
Rye
Rye flour
Safflower (Dyer's thistle / Hong Hua)
Saffron
Sage
Sago (cereals)
Salmon
Salsify
Sea buckthorn
Seacrab
Shark
Sheep's milk
Sheep's milk yoghurt
Shrimp
Shrimps
Skim milk powder
Slug
Sorrel
Sour cream (Schmand) 30% fat
Sour cream 15% fat
Sour milk
Sour milk cheese 20%
Sourdough
Spelled flakes
Spelled grain
Spelled semolina
Spiny lobsters
Spurdog (spiny dogfish, Schillerlocken)

Star anise
Stevia (candyleaf, sweetleaf)
Strawberries
Sugar substitute (sweetener)
Supplementary nutrition
Sweet potato
Tarragon (Estragon)
Tea mixture uric acid lowering
Thyme
Thyme dried
Trout
Tsampa (roasted barley flour)
Turmeric (yellow root)
Turnip
Valerian
Vanilla
Vanilla pod
Vanilla powder
Wakame
Water
Water hot
Wheat
Wheat bulgur
Wheat flakes

Wheat flatbread/pita bread
Wheat flour
Wheat semolina
Wheat semolina for children
Wheatgrass juice
Wheatgrass powder
Whey
White bread (baguette)
White bread (pretzel sticks)
White bread (roll)
White bread (wheat bread)
White breadcrumbs
White dumpling bread (wheat bread cut into chunks)
Whitefish
Wild herbs
Wild strawberries
Wormwood herb
Yam root, yam root tuber
Yarrow
Yarrow tea
Yogi tea
Yogurt (natural, 1.5% fat)

10.3 Use ingredients: little

Acerola fruit nectar or powder
Agar agar (kelp)
Agave nectar
Apple (sour)
Apple (sweet)
Apple juice (natural cloudy)
Apricot jam
Avocado
Bean oil
Bearberry leaf
Beef fillet
Beef meat
Beef meat (calf)
Beef meatbones
Beef Oxtail pieces
Beef soup meat
Berry juice
Bitter melon
Blackberry jam
Blueberry dried
Blueberry jam
Blueberry juice
Borage oil
Buckwheat whole grain
Capers in olive oil
Cauliflower

Caviar
Chestnuts
Chicken egg
Chicken meat
Chicken yolk
Clarified butter
Cocoa
Cooking oil
Corn germ oil
Cow's milk (whole milk 3.5% fat)
Cranberries
Cream sour 20%
Cucumber
Cucumber (spicy cucumber)
Curd cheese 40%
Currant jam (black)
Currant jam (red)
Currant juice (black)
Currants (black)
Currants (red)
Dates dried
Dates red
Deer meat
Deer meat
Deer's Bones
Ducks egg

Edam cheese
Feta cheese
Fig dried
Fish innards
Fish remains
Fish sauce
Fresh cheese
Fresh cheese from soya
Fresh cheese with herbs
Fructose (glucose)
Fruit mix juice
Goat
Goose egg
Grape juice red
Grape juice white
Grapes red
Grapes white
Grapeseed oil
Grass carp
Green spelt
Herring
Hibiscus
Honey
Hop
Horse meat
Kiwi
Kombu seaweed (Saccharina japonica)
Lamb bones
Lamb meat
Lamb shoulder
Linseed oil
Mackerel
Malt
Mango
Mango juice
mango powder
Maple syrup
Margarine
Margarine (diet)
Mold cheese
Mozzarella
Multi-grain bread (gray bread)
Mustard seeds
Mutton
Mutton
Nectarine
Oat flakes roasted
Oat meal
Olive oil
Orange jam
Palm oil
Peaches
Peaches (canned)
Peanut oil

Pear
Pear juice
Pheasant
Pigeon
Pigeon egg
Pineapple
Pineapple (from a can)
Pineapple juice without sugar
Poppy
Pork ham
Pork ham cooked
Pork ham smoked
Pork knuckle
Pork meat
processed cheese 30%
Pumpkin seed oil
Quail
Quail egg
Rabbit
Rabbit (wild)
Rabbit meat
Raisins
Rapeseed oil
Raspberry dried (immature)
Raspberry jam
Rooibos tea
Salt
Salt (herbal)
Sesame oil
Soy flour
Soy noodles
Soy sauce
Soy Tofu
Soy Tofu smoked
Soybean milk
Soybean oil
Spelled (Dark) bread
Spelled wholemeal flour
St. Benedict's thistle, blessed thistle, holy thistle, spotted thistle
Strawberry jam
Strawberry Juice
Sugar - icing sugar
Sugar brown
Sugar candy white
Sugar cane sugar
Sugar fructose - fruit sugar
Sugar glucose - grapes sugar
Sugar Milk Sugar
Sugar molasses
Sugar palm sugar
Sugar white
Sunflower oil
Thistle oil

Tomato
Tomato juice
Tomato paste
Tomato puree
Tonic Water
Truffle
Tuna
Turkey breast meat
Turkey ham
Umeboshi paste
Vanilla sugar natural

Vegetable juice
Vinegar (Apple vinegar)
Vinegar (Red wine vinegar)
Vinegar Aceto Balsamico
Vinegar Aceto Balsamico white
Walnut oil
Wheat germ oil
Wild boar meat
Yeast
Yoghurt vanilla
Yogurt (natural, 3.5% fat)

10.4 Do not use contra-acting foods

Adzuki beans
Agrimony
Almond
Almond marzipan
Almond milk
Almond puree
Anchovy / Sardine
Apricot
Apricot dried
Apricot nectar
Apricots
Apricots juice
Basic recipe for a duck soup
Beans (green, fresh)
Beef bone marrow
Beef heart
Beef heart (calf)
Beef kidney
Beef liver
Beef lungs (calf)
Beef stomach
Beer (alcohol-free)
Beer (alcohol-reduced)
Beer (Pils)
Beer (Top-fermented German dark beer)
Bitter Lemon
Bitter liqueur
Bitter orange peel
Black beans
Black fungus mushroom
Black tea
Blackberry dried (unripe fruit)
Black-eyed peas
Blackthorn (Sloe)
Bocksdorn fruits (Fructus Lycii, goji berry dried
Boletus mushroom
Brazil nuts
Brie cheese

Broad beans (thick beans)
Brown ale
Brussels sprouts
Bush beans
Butter beans white
Camembert
Campari
Carp
Cashews
Champignon
Chanterelle
Chenpi (chinese tangerine bowl)
Cherry
Cherry (sour)
Cherry compote
Cherry juice
Chicken Blood
Chicken heart
Chicken liver
Chicken stomach
Chickpeas
Chili (pod or ground)
Chinese cabbage
Chives
Chocolate
Chocolate (Diabetic)
Clementine
Clementines
Coconut fat
Coconut flakes
Coconut grated
Coconut meat
Coconut milk
Coffee
Cola drink
Cola drink (low calorie)
Cream (30% fat)
Cream sour 30%
Cream, sweet 30%
Crème fraiche cheese

Curry
Curry paste red
Deer's kidneys
Duck (heart)
Duck (slaughtered)
Dyer's broom herb
Eel
Eel smoked
Emmental cheese
Evening primrose oil
Fernet Branca (herbal bitter liqueur)
French beans
Gail plum
Garam Masala powder
Garlic
Ginger fresh
Ginger oil
Ginger powder
Ginseng liqueur
Goat and sheep's blood
Goat and sheep's brain
Goat and sheep's liver
Goat and sheep's stomach
Goose
Goose blood
Goose fat
Goose parts
Gorgonzola
Gouda cheese
Grapefruit (Pomelo)
Grapefruit dried peel
Grapefruit juice
Greengage
Hazelnuts
Honey wine (Met)
Horehound leaves
Kaki plum
Kidney beans (red)
Lamb kidneys
Lamb liver
Leek
Lemon
Lemon juice
Lemon peel
Lentils
Lentils black
Lentils red
Lentils yellow
Lima beans
Lime
Linseed
Linseed (crushed)
Lychee liqueur
Manioc flour

Martini
Mayonnaise 50%
Mayonnaise 80%
Mirabelle plum
Miso paste (soy bean paste)
Mixed Pickles
Morel (black, dried)
Morel, dried
Mu Erh Mushroom
Muesli
Mung bean
Mung bean sprouting
Mustard
Mustard Dijon
Mustard medium hot
Mustard sweet
Noodles (whole grain) with egg
Oat flakes (whole grain)
Olives
Olives green
Onion (shallot)
Onion (spring onion)
Onion read
Onion white
Orange
Orange dried peel
Orange grated peel
Orange juice
Orange peel
Oyster mushroom
Oyster shell powder
Parmesan
Peanut (roasted)
Peanut butter
Peanuts
Peas
Peas, green
Pepper Cayenne
Pepper powder (hot)
Pepper white (ground)
Peppercorns
Pepperoni
Pepperoni, red, pitted, halved
Pepperoni, yellow, pitted, halved
Peppers
Peppers (rose peppers)
Peppers (sweet)
Peppers powder
Pickle
Pig blood
Pine nuts
Pinto beans speckled
Pistachios
Plum

Plum dried
Plums
Pork Bacon
Pork brain
Pork fat (lard)
Pork heart
Pork kidneys
Pork Lard
Pork liver
Pork lung
Pork marrow bones
Pork sausage (Bratwurst) Pork skin
Pork stomach
Pork/beef sausage (smoked)
Pork's intestine
Prosecco
Psyllium seed
Puff pastry
Pumpernickel (dark bread)
Pumpkin seeds
Rabbit liver
Radish
Radish (white, green, purple-red)
Radish horseradish
Red cabbage
Red wine
Reishi mushroom
Rice (whole grain)
Rice black
Rice wild (nature rice)
Rum
Rye wholemeal bread
Sake
Sauerkraut (cutted cabbage fermented)
Savory
Savoy cabbage / kale
Sea cucumber

Sesame oil roasted
Sesame paste (Tahini)
Sesame, black
Sesame, white
Sherry (whine)
Shiitake, dried
Sour cherries
Soy cream
Soya Cuisine (soy cream)
Soybeans
Soybeans, black
Soybeans, blacks, fermented
Soybeans, yellow
Spirit
Sunflower seeds
Tabasco
Tangerine
Toast bread (whole grain)
Tomato dried
Trout (smoked)
Umeboshi plums (Japanese apricots)
Walnuts
Walnuts roasted
Wheat beer
Wheat bran
Wheat flour whole grain
Wheat/Rye/Gray-black bread with yeast
White beans
White cabbage
White wine
Whole grain bread
Wholemeal bread with whole grains
Wholemeal flour
Wild garlic (garlic spinach)
Wormwood
Yew nut

11 Complementary

11.1 Blond plantain, desert Indianwheat, blond psyllium

Plantago ovata
Preparation: Cooking addition
Moistens intestines, softens stool. Dissolves mucus.
In the outer layer of the seed shells are mucilage, which swell in the colon with the help of water. This leads to an increase in volume in the intestine, which in turn stimulates the activity of the digestive organ and its contents transported faster. The slime and fat oil also exert a kind of

lubrication effect, whereby the intestinal contents is transported easier. Whole or crushed Indian psyllium as well as the pure seed shells serve as a mild laxative. Very important: drink a lot!
Dosage: 1-2 teaspoons per meal: can be used by the spoonful or as a food additive. Very important: drink a lot!
Note: Psyllium should be taken ½ to 1 hour before or after taking other medicines, as otherwise the absorption of other medicines from the gastrointestinal tract may be delayed.

11.2 Centaurium (centaury)

Centaurium, herb.
Preparation: Healing tea (infusion)
Clarifies stomach heat, dries moisture. Tonifies Spleen-Qi and Stomach-Qi, moves Liver-Qi and Intestinal-Qi. Derives moisture-heat and heat.
Dosage: Pour 2 teaspoons of the tea into 250 ml of boiling water and leave for 10 minutes. Then sieve.
Drink 2 to 3 cups per day as needed.
Note: Do not use during stomach ulcers.

11.3 Hop

Humulus lupulus
Preparation: Healing tea (infusion)
Clears heart-void heat, soothes Shen, regulates and moves Qi, lowers Liver-Yang, tonifies Stomach-Qi, cools Heat.
The hop flowers contain lupulin and resins which are composed of humulones, lupolones and bitter substances such as hop bitter acid and acylphloroglucides. In addition, an essential oil and various tannins.
Dosage: Daily dose 0.5 g of the cones or 1-2 ml of the tincture. Pour about 0,5 g of the crushed hop cones with boiling water and pass through a tea strainer after 10-15 minutes.

11.4 Lady's mantle

Herba Alchemillae
Preparation: Healing tea (infusion)
Uterus strengthening, astringent. Dries moisture, clears heat, diuretic, lowers emptiness-heat, cooling.
For a tea use about 2 teaspoons of dried lady's mantle herb and pour over 150 ml of boiling water. The infusion is allowed to draw for 10 minutes and then he is off. Always prepare the tea fresh and drink. In case of complaints, the tea can be drunk
 three to five times a day. For diarrheal diseases should be dispensed

with sugar in tea, as it can increase diarrhea. Lady's mantle is usually well tolerated and can therefore be used over a longer period of time.
Dosage: Pour 2 teaspoons of dried tea with 150 ml of boiling water. Let it draw for 10 minutes and strain.
Note: A Japanese study has shown that the tannins (ellagitannins) can have a tumor-inhibiting effect. Regularly applied, the mantle can thus prevent female cancers.

11.5 Senna leaves

Sennae folium
Preparation: Cold extract (macerate)
Clarifying heat in the gut, laxing, stopping bleeding. Increases the blood flow to the abdominal arteries.
Dosage: 1-2 g of dried leaves for macerate; 1-2 ml tincture.
Note: Only for short-term use (1 to 2 weeks), as the effect occurs after a latency period of 10-12 hours after ingestion. Take before going to bed.

11.6 Turmeric

Curcuma longa
Preparation: Cooking addition
Eliminates moisture-heat, dissipates mucus-heat from the lungs.
Eliminates heat from the stomach and intestines. Moves qi and blood.
Active ingredients: eth. Oil, bitter substances, curcumin, starch.
Turmeric or Tumeric - Has achieved impressive success in the treatment of carcinogens and mutagens in laboratory animals.
Concentrated turmeric showed an increase in the glutathione S-transferase enzymes, which are essential for life and liver detoxification.

Medical applications: Amenorrhoea, anemia, arthritis, asthma, blood clots, cancer, candida, catarrh, anabolic, cough, dysentery, dysmenorrhea, eczema, winds, gallbladder disease, gallstones, gastritis, heart disease, hepatitis, high cholesterol, indigestion, irritable Intestines, jaundice, liver detoxification, liver protection, nausea, obesity, cerebral catarrh, skin diseases, including parasitic skin infections, traumas, urinary tract diseases, tumors of the uterus.
Properties: Alterative, analgesic, antibiotic, anti-coagulant (inhibits blood clotting) antifungal, anti-inflammatory, antioxidant, antiseptic, aromatic, astringent, cholagogue, circulation stimulating, digestive, the entry of the menstrual period promoting agent, liver-strengthening, stimulant, supports wound healing.
Note: When blockade bile ducts or gallstones should be dispensed turmeric.

11.7 Wormwood

Artemisia absinthium, herb.
Preparation: Healing tea (infusion)
Strengthens Spleen-Qi and Stomach-Qi, moves Liver-Qi, regulates bile flow, dissipating Moisture-Heat and Heat, regulating the uterus.
Vermouth - Not only used to eliminate worms; it is also a highly effective liver and digestive aid. He also helps to remove blockages that produce a lethargic menstruation. It is always best to take this herbal remedy in conjunction with other herbs.

Medical applications: anemia, arthritis, bloating, circulatory system, colds, constipation, depression, edema, earache, fever, gynecology, wind, gallbladder, gallstones, gout, heartburn, hepatitis, jaundice, kidney disease, morning sickness, nausea, obesity, parasites, Rheumatism, stomach ailments, worms.

Properties: Abortive, alterative, appetite promoting, wormer, antibiotic, anti-depressant, anti-inflammatory, antipyretic, antiseptic, aromatic, bittertonikum, anti-flatulence, cholagogue, digestive, menstrual enhancer, stomach-strengthening, wormer.
Dosage: 1 tsp. To 1 / 2l water
Note: Do not use in pregnancy. It is always best to take this herbal remedy in conjunction with other herbs.

12 Basics of Nutrition

The basic principles of nutrition described herein are general recommendations. They are not aimed at a specific form of therapy. Recommendations concerning a therapy have priority.

12.1 Nutrition

Regular meals in a relaxed atmosphere. A warm breakfast is considered a good start into the day.
The main meals ought to be taken for lunch – supper in the early evening. Pay attention to feeling hungry or sated: don't eat too much nor remain hungry is the rule
Prepare the meals freshly from natural, regional products. Frozen, heat-conserved, industrially prepared or foodstuffs cooked in the microwave oven are rejected.
Choice of foodstuffs according to the season: more cooling food in summer, more warming food in winter.
Eat cooked food at least twice a day. Food and drinks ought to be lukewarm, never ice-cold or hot.
Raw vegetables, briefly cooked vegetables, freshly squeezed juices and mineral water are not recommended. Milk and dairy products are only included in the diet if they don't cause problems.
Don't use therapeutic recipes over a longer period without consulting your doctor or therapist.

Varied food
Enjoy the diversity of foodstuffs. Characteristics of a balanced nutrition are variety, suitable combination and a balanced quantity of rich and low energy foodstuffs (on one hand avoiding undersupply with essential nutrients and on the other hand to take to many undesirable substances).

A lot of Cereal Products - and Potatoes
Bread, pasta, rice, cereal flakes (best wholemeal) as well as potatoes contain almost no fat, but many vitamins, mineral nutrients, trace elements, roughage and secondary plant substances. These foodstuffs ought to be taken with low-fat side dishes.

Vegetables and Fruit – „Take Five" every day ...
5 portions of vegetables and fruit a day, as fresh as possible, briefly cooked, or maybe one portion as a juice – ideal as a side dish to every meal as well as snack between meals: Thus a lot of vitamins, mineral nutrients as well as roughage and secondary plant substances

Daily milk and dairy products
Milk and Dairy Products every Day, once or twice per Week Fish; meat, sausages as well as eggs moderately. These foodstuffs contain valuable nutrients like calcium in the milk, iodine selenium and omega-3 fat acids in saltwater fish. Meat is favorable due to its high content of disposable iron and the vitamins B1, B6 and B12. Quantities of 300 – 600 g meat and sausage per week are sufficient. Prefer low-fat products, especially in meat- and dairy products.

Low-fat and fatty Foodstuffs
Fat supplies us with essential fat acids and fatty foodstuffs contain also fat-soluble vitamins. Fat is high in energy; therefore much fat in the food may cause overweight, possibly also cancer. Too many saturated fat acids may further a tendency for cardio-vascular diseases in the long term. Prefer vegetable oils and fats (e.g. rapeseed-, olive-, soya-oils and solid fats produced therefrom). Beware of invisible fat in meat- and dairy products, pastry and sweets as well as in fast-food and convenience foods. 70 – 90 g fat per day is sufficient.

Moderately Sugar and Salt
Take sugar and foods/drinks containing various kinds of sugar (e.g. glucose syrup) only occasionally. Use herbs and spices as well as a little salt creatively. Prefer salt containing iodine.

Plenty of Liquids
Water is absolutely essential. Drink 1-2 l liquids every day. Prefer water (with or without gas) and other low-calorie drinks. Alcoholic drinks should not be taken.

Tasty Dishes, carefully cooked
Cook the meals with as low temperatures and as short as possible, using little water and fat – this preserves the original taste, keeps the nutrients intact and prevents the production of harmful compounds.

Take time and enjoy the food
Take your Time and enjoy your Food
Eating consciously helps to eat right. The eye enjoys food, too. It's fun, invites to enjoy varied dishes and stimulates the feeling of satiety.

Watch your Weight and stay in Motion
A balanced diet and a lot of exercise and sport (30 – 60 min/day) are a healthy combination. The right weight furthers well-being and health. Thermals, directional effectiveness, digestive power

There are various criteria for judging the effectiveness of herbs and foodstuffs.

The use of certain herbs and ingredients is based on observations of the effects on the body which these foodstuffs, herbs and spices show after having eaten them. The medical science has developed following system: Every ingredient or herb has a directional effectiveness. Furthermore, there are herbs which have a special effect on certain organs.

The basic condition for a healthy metabolism is to obtain sufficient energy from food and that the digestive process doesn't use too much energy. An easily digestible meal makes content and sated, doesn't cause flatulence and fatigue after the meal. The perfect spices increase the healthiness of our meals. Very often, just small doses of herbs and spices will suffice. They are not used to make us sated, but to help our digestive organs to digest the food.

12.2 Recipes

The recipes list the ingredients to be used and the cooking instructions show how the dish is prepared. The list of ingredients shows the concerned quantities as well as the relevance for the therapy. If you find „less than mentioned", try to comply or find an alternative from the „list of recommended foodstuffs". Mostly it shall result just in a small change of taste when you simply avoid this ingredient.

Mild cooking methods: boiling, stewing, poaching, steaming
Strong cooking methods: barbecuing, roasting, frying, smoking
Balanced cooking methods: deep-frying, baking brick
Deep-freezing and warming in the microwave oven should be avoided (denaturalization).

12.3 Foodstuffs

Foodstuffs have an effect on body and soul like medicinal herbs, only a very much milder one. Dietary advice is mainly based on regional foodstuffs. The knowledge about the effects of each foodstuff and the knowledge, when which foodstuff shall be used, is based on the orthodox school of medicine. Use ecologic-organic products, if possible. As everything should be cooked for a long time due to a better digestability and very rarely eaten raw, the food agrees with everyone.

The classification of the foodstuffs according to their effect on the body is the basis in order to achieve a harmonious status of health.

Dietary advisors do not recommend certain foodstuffs for everyone. The individual diet is tailor-made for the individual constitution.

Buy only fresh and ripe fruit and vegetables. You ought to leave unripe fruit and vegetables and such with brown spots and wilted leaves behind in the market. In this case take deep-frozen goods (never ready-to-serve dishes!). Fruit and vegetables are deep-frozen immediately after harvesting and often contain more vitamins and minerals than the goods from the vegetable shelf. Whereas conserved or tinned goods contain very much less biological substances. Also, salt, sugar and others are mostly added to the latter. Never leave the foodstuffs in the water after washing them to avoid that many vital substances get drowned. Clean salads, fruit and vegetables immediately before serving.

Please make sure of the hygienic processing of foodstuffs. Clean your salads, fruit and vegetables carefully. When cooking with meat, prepare all ingredients first and then process the meat products. Clean the worktop and tools very carefully. Wooden surfaces ought to be treated with a mild disinfectant regularly in order to reduce germination.

Store fruit and vegetables separately, if possible. Harvested fruit and vegetables are still alive and emit e.g. ethylene gas, which makes other products ripen and age faster. Keep meat and fish in the closed packaging or store them in the fridge in closed containers.

12.4 Herbs

There are some basic rules for storing medicinal herbs. On principle, herbs must be protected from direct sunlight, humidity and heat.

Containers for the storage of herbs may be glasses, ceramic jars and even plastic containers. However, plastic is a rather unsuitable material and should only be a short-term solution. In case of glass containers, use a dark material.

Medicinal herbs cannot be kept for any long period. The shelf life of herbs is limited. However, it can be prolonged with suitable storage. The place should be dark, rather cool and absolutely dry. A wooden medicine cabinet, placed not directly next to a source of heat, would be ideal. Never buy large quantities of herbs so as not to have to throw them away. Label the container with the name of the herb and the date of harvesting or processing.

13 Other dietic-books

The following syndromes of dietetics, TCM or for a therapy supplement for cancer are available.

<u>Dietetics</u>

E001. Nutrition of the infant - baby food
E002. Nutrition during lactation
E003. Nutrition in old age
E004. Nutrition of children and adolescents
E005. Nutrition of athletes
E006. Light weight
E007. Pregnancy
E008. Full food

Protein and electrolyte - kidneys
E009. (hemodialysis) dialysis treatment
E010. Acute renal failure
E011. Chronic renal insufficiency
E012. Nephrotic syndrome
E013. Kidney stones (nephrolithiasis)

Gastrointestinal tract - pancreas
E014. Acute pancreatitis (inflammation of the pancreas)
E015. Chronic pancreatitis (inflammation of the pancreas)

Gastrointestinal tract - small intestine and large intestine
E016. Acute obstipation (constipation)
E017. Chronic obstipation (constipation)
E018. Colon irritabile
E019. Diverticulitis
E020. Acquired lactose intolerance (lactose malabsorption)
E021. Fructose malabsorption
E022. Glutensensitive enteropathy (celiac disease)
E023. Colectomy
E024. Short Bowel Syndrome

Gastrointestinal tract - liver, gallbladder, bile ducts
E025. Acute and chronic hepatitis (inflammation of the liver)
E026. Cholelithiasis (bile stones)
E027. fatty liver
E028. cirrhosis

Gastrointestinal tract - Stomach and duodenal intestine
E029. Acute gastritis
E030. Chronic gastritis
E031. Stomach bleeding
E032. Ulcus ventriculi and duodenal ulcer
E033. Condition after gastric surgery

Gastrointestinal tract - oral cavity and esophagus
E034. Stomatitis
E035. Esophageal carcinoma (esophageal cancer)
E036. Refluosophagitis (heartburn)

Special diseases
E037. Phenylketonuria (PKU)
E038. Rheumatic joint diseases

Metabolism
E039. Obesity (overweight)
E040. Diabetes mellitus
E041. Eating disorders (underweight)

Fat metabolism
E042. Hypercholesterolaemia (increased cholesterol level)
E043. Hepatic Encephalopathy

Heart and circulation
E044. Arteriosclerosis (arterial calcification)
E045. Heart insufficiency
E046. Hypertension
E047. Hyperuricaemia and gout

Changed nutrient requirements
E048. In case of fever
E049. For malignant diseases
E050. After burns
E051. Radiation and chemotherapy

CANCER
E100. Pancreatic cancer
E101. Bladder cancer
E102. Blood cancer (leukemia)
E103. Breast cancer
E104. Colorectal cancer
E105. Gastric cancer
E106. Kidney cancer
E107. Esophageal cancer

TCM
E200. Bladder - moisture heat in the bladder
E201. Bladder - moisture and cold in the bladder
E202. Bladder - emptiness and cold in the bladder
E203. Large intestine - external cold affects the large intestine
E204. Large intestine - moisture heat in the large intestine
E205. Large intestine - heat blocks the intestine II acute
E206. Large intestine - dryness of the colon
E207. Large intestine - Yang deficiency (cold)
E208. Heart - Blood insufficiency
E209. Heart - Blood stagnation
E210. Heart - Fire
E211. Heart - Hot mucus clogs the heart pores

E212. Heart - Cold mucus clogs the heart pores
E213. Heart - Qi deficiency
E214. Heart - Yang deficiency
E215. Heart - Yin deficiency
E216. Liver - Ascending Liver Yang
E217. Liver - Blood deficiency
E218. Liver - Blood stagnation
E219. Liver - Moisture heat in liver and gall bladder
E220. Liver - Fire
E221. Liver - Gall bladder Qi-Empty
E222. Liver - Cold in the liver meridian
E223. Liver - Qi stagnation
E224. Liver - Wind
E225. Liver - Wind with ascending liver Yang
E226. Liver - Wind with blood anemic
E227. Liver - Wind with extreme heat
E228. Lung - Qi deficiency
E229. Lung - Mucus-moisture in the lungs
E230. Lung - Mucus-heat in the lungs
E231. Lung - Mucus-cold in the lungs
E232. Lung - Dryness of the lungs
E233. Lung - Wind-heat attacks the lungs
E234. Lung - Wind-cold affects the lungs
E235. Lung - Yin deficiency
E236. Stomach - Bloodstagnation
E237. Stomach - Fire
E238. Stomach - Cold with liquid
E239. Stomach - Nutrition stagnation
E240. Stomach - Qi deficiency
E241. Stomach - Rebellious Qi
E242. Stomach - Yin Emptiness
E243. Spleen - Heat and moisture attack the spleen
E244. Spleen - Coldness and moisture affects the spleen
E245. Spleen - Qi deficiency
E246. Spleen - Qi deficiency + Declining spleen Qi
E247. Spleen - Qi deficiency + spleen does not control the blood
E248. Spleen - Yang deficiency
E249. Kidney - Heart and kidney no longer communicate
E250. Kidney - Jing deficiency
E251. Kidney - Kidneys cannot receive the Qi
E252. Kidney - Qi is not stable
E253. Kidney - Yang deficiency
E254. Kidney - Yin deficiency

For further information visit di-book.com.

14 EBNS - Software for nutritional counseling

The main task of the database is to create personalized nutritional advice for each patient individually. The database was developed for Dietetics

and Traditional Chinese Medicine.
The Database supports training and advices in the daily work routine.

The computer program provides lists of recipes, ingredients and herbs, which are given to the client. individually adjustable according to patient's request from whole food to vegetarians (lacto, ovo, ...). For every register there is an information sheet which can be given to the client. All texts can be individually designed.

The syndromes can be combined and result in an intersection of the recommended recipes and ingredients. The automated diagnosis for the TCM enables you to check your experience during the training as well as to confirm your diagnosis in the working day. You select several predefined symptoms and have the program automatically display the relevant syndromes.

How to work with the database:
Select the patient / client, select one or more of the syndromes you diagnosed and print the folder.

You can change all values, create new symptoms or syndromes, develop recipes, change or adapt ingredients and herbs to your findings. In simple client management, all relevant data about the person is stored. You get an overview of the past diagnoses and the development of the course of the disease.

As a consultant you save a lot of time when you print out the recipe, food and herbal lists for the recognized syndromes and give them to the clients. You can use this time for a personal conversation. With the database, dieticians and nutritionists can view the nutrients and trace elements for each recipe and develop recipes for syndromes even with suggested ingredients.

All recipe and grocery lists can also be ordered from me as a combination of several diseases. I wish all readers good luck, health and happiness in life.
More information can be found at www.ebns.at.
Volunteer: www.krebsinfo.at
Josef Miligui